HOW TO

CONTROL

YOUR **BUSINESS** AND YOUR **LIFE**

Proven Secrets

TO CREATING HIGHLY PRODUCTIVE TEAMS

KEITH LEE

Contents

PREFACE
But Who Has the Time?

If you're a business owner with employees and one of the following describes you, this book is for you:

- I have become a slave to my business. It seems like I'm always responding to things and taking care of problems. I have no time for myself. This is not fun.
- My business runs well, but if it ran smoother and I didn't have to do so many "regular everyday menial things" then I could work on actually improving and growing the business.
- My business is great, but I'm always looking for ways to improve our efficiency and effectiveness.

Like most who have picked up this book, you're likely an accomplished, driven, business owner or top manager... and since you're still reading you know that if you could control your business better you could accomplish even more. That's what this book is all about - showing you exactly how to take control of your business with Step-By-Step, Easy to Implement Systems.

You will take TOTAL control of your business when you create systems to control your business. **But Who Has Time To Create Those Systems?**

You can start from scratch, but the good news is you don't need to. I'll show you how to use what's already been developed to implement the systems you need in your business.

You have undoubtedly been part of this conversation. Whenever business owners get together the conversation always

1

gets around to the headaches. Trying to get staff functioning as an effective team, at a high level as individuals, and in general, getting things done right consistently by implementing systems instead of fighting fires and fixing mistakes.

In fact, many business owners decide they just don't want the headaches anymore and decide not to grow their business.

It should not be that way. The reality is, when managed properly, your employees become the ultimate leverage, job security and wealth for YOU! But I need to warn you, it will be a bit uncomfortable when you get together with those business owners complaining about their employees because you'll no longer be one of them.

One of my favorite mentors, Dan Kennedy says,
"All wealth is based on systems."

In *The E-Myth Revisited* Michael Gerber says,
"Let systems run the business and people run the systems. People come and go, but systems remain constant."

I agree with both Gerber and Kennedy and add,
"For the business owner, systems set you free."

CHAPTER 1
Systems Set You Free

When you have the proper systems in place in your business, you'll create time freedom, physical freedom, mind freedom and financial freedom for yourself.

Time Freedom

With the proper systems in place you'll have time to work on the really important things in your business rather than spending your time working on mundane, everyday duties. For me, that means spending my time starting four other businesses, acquiring eleven competitors, and acquiring two complementary businesses. It also means that I spend my time on what I want to do, not what I have to do.

I love marketing, and I think it's the most important skill any independent business owner can acquire. The systems we have in place in my various businesses allow me to spend the majority of my time on marketing for my businesses. In fact, if you knew me and knew I had written a business book, you would assume it was about marketing. The reality is that the management system I developed in 1992 has allowed me to become extremely good at marketing because I don't spend my time managing. Two of my five businesses teach direct response advertising and marketing to business owners.

The management system frees me up so that with five businesses I spend less than one hour a week "managing my team."

In 1991, I was the guy I discussed in the Preface who had become a slave to my business. It seemed like I was always responding to things and taking care of problems. I had no time for myself and was having no fun. Since I developed the system in 1992, I take about 10 weeks of vacation each year, have grown the original business by leaps and bounds, started 4 more businesses, didn't miss anything when my kids were growing up... **and I am having fun!**

Physical Freedom

Physical freedom is similar to time freedom, but it's important to understand the difference. Time freedom is having the time to go and do what you want. Physical freedom, in regards to your work, is being able to work where you want.

When you need to be at work to "keep an eye on things" or "take care of things" or whatever, you don't have physical freedom. When you have the proper systems in place, you have the freedom to **not** go to the office. When I'm at my Seattle house, I usually come in to the office. As I said, I spend most of my time on marketing and when it comes to marketing, I'm more productive in my office at work than at home.

When it comes to writing, I'm as productive or more productive in my home office or at our vacation house in Montana. So I often write at home in Seattle, or at our vacation house in Montana. There is something about writing for a couple hours in the morning and then stepping off the deck to fly fish for a couple hours that gets the juices flowing.

Physical freedom means you don't need to be in the office to "keep an eye on things" or "take care of things."

In fact, when you have the right systems in place,
and **buy-in** from your team,
the business will continue to improve
whether you're there or not.

Mind Freedom

When I installed the systems I needed so that I didn't have to continually work on problems, or "issues" fixing this or that, and being the King Solomon decision maker, I was amazed at the explosion of great ideas I had to grow the business.

While this mind freedom was fabulous, it was just as important that I no longer had to solve everything. I didn't need to be the all-knowing, all-seeing, and all-powerful one who discovered every new idea, solved every problem, and found the secret to capitalizing on every opportunity. When your entire team **buys-in** to your vision, the ideas, solutions and opportunities to improve explode.

I'm a big fan of Michael Gerber. With that being said, my biggest problem with the franchise model as described in Michael Gerber's book, *The E-Myth Revisited*, is that the improvement in your business is dependent almost entirely on you... and you just ain't that smart.

I know a lot about every job we do in our businesses and I certainly know the outcome I expect. But added up, the combined knowledge of our warehouse people far surpasses what I know about warehouse operations. The same is true in our tech support department, purchasing, accounting, etc. When those people are empowered to continually improve your business, your business will continually improve.

5

We've all seen motivational posters with slogans like, "When **WE** all work together, we all win together," and "Together we achieve more." These are great. There is nothing wrong with posters, but far too often, they are just slogans and pictures with a management system that does nothing to support them.

When you create a management system that empowers people, you will get Buy-In, your business will continue to improve every day, and you will have mind freedom.

Financial Freedom

When it comes time to sell your business and you're critical to that business, how much is it going to be worth?

You know the answer – **NOT MUCH**.

But what if… it comes time to sell your business and you're not critical to the operations, and in fact the business actually improves whether you're there or not? What's it worth now?

You know the answer – **LOTS**.

When you empower your team and have the proper systems in place, you will not be critical to the operations of your business, plus your business will continue to improve whether you're there or not.

CHAPTER 2
Playing Pinball

My Make-You-Happy Management System didn't just come about overnight. Even though I graduated with a degree in Business Administration from the prestigious, private University of Puget Sound, I certainly didn't learn this system in college. It actually got its start out of a huge amount of frustration. I was the guy I described earlier who had become a slave to my business. It seemed like I was always responding to things and taking care of problems. I had no time for myself. It was not fun.

In 1991, my business was nicely profitable, but I had decided that I didn't want it to grow anymore. It seemed like the only things that grew as fast as my business were my headaches, and I sure as heck didn't want any more employees... talk about headaches. I might as well have been a babysitter.

I really think some of the people at American Retail Supply liked playing pinball with my blood pressure. "Hey, we haven't seen Keith's face turn red for a while. Let's bring him a problem and watch him turn red."

"Hey, I bet I can make Keith's face turn red faster than you. What's the record? 2.5 seconds?"

"Oh yeah? I can keep it red longer!"

"Yeah, but I do it more often."

Whether you feel like I did, just know that if you didn't need to take care of so many menial everyday things, or simply understand that you could achieve more by getting everyone on the same side of the table working together, this management system is for you.

7

In the early 1990's, I had a 10,000 square foot warehouse at American Retail Supply, and I was burned out. Today I own 5 businesses with a combined total of 80,000 square feet. Because of the systems I've put in place, I spend all of my time on important things, not menial things.

I live in the Seattle area and own a manufacturing facility in Bend, Oregon that builds high-end hardwood displays, but I don't know where the "ON" switch is for a single piece of machinery.

My company, American Retail Supply, has three large sales and distribution centers (70,000 square feet total) in Seattle, Denver and Honolulu, but I can't enter an order properly, enter a purchase order correctly, or pull an order.

I do know how to run the reports that I need to work **on** my businesses, and I check my cash position and other important numbers daily. I've **eliminated Worthless Performance Reviews** that everyone despises, and replaced them with **Personal Development Interviews** that everyone loves, and actually get results (Wouldn't you rather **develop** people than review them?)

I am the marketing guy, and I do the things that multiply me, including the strategic acquisition of 11 competitors and starting 4 businesses that complement my original business. I have 47 team members in five locations across the country, and my headaches are now gone.

What happened? How did I go from a guy who didn't want to expand his business, who had more headaches than he could handle, to a guy whose business has grown dramatically, added four more businesses, loves his work, has the time he wants to spend with his wife, kids, and grandkids, and has time for his many hobbies?

Before 1992, when I went on vacation, I never felt like I got away. It never failed! I either had to work or got called to solve a work-related problem while on vacation. My definition of a great vacation was one without interruptions, but I was always coming back to a pot load of problems.

Now, since 1995, when I go on vacation, I never get interrupted. I come back refreshed and excited to get back to work. Instead of problems, I come back to a business running as well, or better, than when I left.

A couple years ago, I went on a 3-week Mediterranean cruise, with no cell phone and no email. I told my Vice President of Operations the ship I was taking. I told her "You'll have to figure out how to get in touch with me if you need me." I knew she wouldn't need me. Like I said, since around 1995 when I go on vacation, **I never get interrupted.**

How does the business get better while you're gone?

It's the system. As you'll see, the entire system is designed for continuous improvement whether you're there or not.

Here are just a few examples of what happened in my business while I was on that 3-week Mediterranean Cruise.

While I was gone, the office team decided to have a surprise, "thank-you" breakfast for the warehouse team. Here's the email our warehouse manager sent to the office staff team after the unexpected treat.

9

The breakfast and lunch were absolutely wonderful. What we'll keep in our hearts forever is the card. This was all very special from you folks and we'll always remember it. What a statement you made. Thank you from the warehouse team. We think you too are very special and do a lot to make our work easier, but we can't cook...thanks again.

Doug Havey

Here is a voice mail message I returned to.

"My name is Josh Flipner. I'm the manager of Elger Bay Grocery - a small convenience store, gas station, and gift shop on Camano Island. I ordered a copy of the book "The Simple Truths of Service" through your newsletter, and I wanted to let you know that it was amazing and everything you said in the newsletter was 100% correct. I'm really glad you guys put that in there so we had the opportunity to get it.

Here's a card I got from Jeannine Camp from The Groom Room in Ewa Beach, Hawaii while I was on the cruise.

Dear Mr Lee,

I had to write to you and express complete happiness and thankfulness for your staff in Honolulu. First of all I would like to applaud Gary - for his care and great attitude. He not only took excellent care of me at the initial visit to your store but the follow up has been very much appreciated. Gary is a great rep for your company. I hope to do a lot of business with American over time. I want to make mention of Beth, a woman that went out of her way to help and also of the delivery man Martino. You have been blessed with these 3 people in your employ -- Thought you should know.

And another note from Paula Nordby at The Village Shoppe in Enumclaw, Washington...

As always, your service was right on – thanks. And thanks for the wonderful Marketing Tips of the Week - I look forward to them each week.

So what happened? How do you create a business with that type of caring for clients and co-workers? How is it that I used to dread coming back from vacation to a bunch of problems? Now, not only don't I dread coming back, but also I consistently come back to great news.

What happened is that I developed a management system that made me more money, made my job infinitely easier and more enjoyable... a system that our employees love and in fact led to us being named "The Best Small Business To Work For In Washington State" by *Washington CEO Magazine*. It's a management system that creates great clients who love doing business with you. At the same time it gives you, the owner, more time to work on the important things in your business: more time for your family, more time for your friends, more time for yourself and it is simply a lot more fun.

CHAPTER 3
Bobby Radel's Dad

They say necessity is the mother of invention, and in this case it's true.

My story of discovering the secrets to my management system goes back to 1966. The #1 song on the Billboard Charts is *The Sound of Silence* by Simon and Garfunkel. The Rolling Stones appear on the Ed Sullivan Show.

I'm 12 years old, and I'm up to bat. It's the bottom of the 6th with two outs. (We played 6 innings). The perennial powerhouse Skyway Merchants are up on us 5-4. Bobby Radel is on second. Danny Malner is on third. I'm an OK ballplayer batting 6th in the lineup.

HUGE... Randy Anderson is on the mound for the Merchants. The Randy Anderson I remember reminds me of the Seattle Mariners pitcher Randy Johnson in 1989. He's big, he's scary, **and he's wild!**

It's OK. He's wild so he'll probably walk me, and I'll be off the hook. I just need to make sure I don't get hit.

"Steee-rike one." That's OK.

"Steee-rike two." Oh crap... I can't just stand here and strike out on three pitches and not swing.

I'm swinging at the next pitch regardless.

Yikes!!! I HIT IT!!! It's going over the 1st baseman's head – "STAY FAIR... STAY FAIR... STAY FAIR!" Holy cow, Malner and Radel both score! I DID IT!

I'm the hero. We all celebrate. It's time to go home.

13

There goes Bobby Radel with his dad's arm draped over his shoulder, talking about the game. It's time for me to walk home... alone.

I climb over the back fence, run through the back door and yell, "Mom, I knocked in the winning run. We beat the Merchants!" Mom replies, "That's great, Keith. Wash up for dinner."

"You have only one life,
and no one else will live it for you.
Shouldn't you take the time right now to figure
out what that life is all about?"
~ Harry Browne

Today, at 59 years old, it's clear that I figured out 'what that life is all about' that summer.

I was going to be Bobby Radel's dad

Bobby Radel's Dad was at every game we played - football, baseball, basketball – from grade school through high school. At Skyway Park, he always stood next to the bleachers towards the back. Every time Bobby went to bat, he gave a quick look at his dad and his dad gave him a "thumbs up."

Don't get me wrong. We had good times. I had great parents. They made sure our family achieved the American Dream: their kids having had more opportunities than they had. Heck, before dinner, at 12 years old, I was playing baseball in the afternoon and not milking cows at 20 below, like my dad did.

The address on my birth certificate is
#9 Fink Trailer Court, Minot, ND

14

For the first two years of my life, my Dad, Mom, older brother Ron, and I lived in an 8-foot wide by 26-foot long trailer, and the 26 feet included the hitch.

Pursuing the American dream, we moved from Minot to Seattle for the opportunity, and my Dad got it. He went to work at Carnation making ice cream. He eventually became foreman for the ice cream plant. Mom got a part-time job at Sears. We had a lot of good times, but I mostly remember Dad working.

At Carnation they got 5-gallon metal cans of syrup to make flavored ice cream. My Dad saw all of those empty cans going to the dump, and he saw that local nurseries were using cans similar to them for pots. He asked the boss if he could take the empty cans home. He cleaned them, straightened them out with a hammer and anvil, and went around to the nurseries to see what they would pay.

The nurseries were receptive, and Dad started taking all of the empty buckets from Carnation. He rented a garage to straighten and clean them, creating a third income for the family. He was at the garage most evenings, and he was providing for his family.

Yes, we were achieving the American Dream. The next generation, my brother, sister and I had it much better than our parents' generation.

Thanks, Mom and Dad!

Fast forward to 1992 - I had been managing American Retail Supply for eleven years and I was Bobby Radel's Dad. Travis, my son, was twelve and Jenny was ten. I spent all the time any dad could on being a dad, and for me, a big part of being a responsible dad was being a good breadwinner. In eleven years, American Retail Supply had grown dramatically.

But…

CHAPTER 4
Burned Out

It seemed like all I did at work was take care of problems and then run home and be Bobby Radel's Dad. I didn't have any time for myself: physically, mentally, or spiritually.

But I saw a light at the end of the tunnel. It's amazing to me that when you keep at it, keep looking, and not give up, the answer somehow arrives. Just as I was saying, "I really don't want my business to grow. The only things that seem to grow as fast as my business are my headaches." I found the answer. Well, I didn't find it – I created it.

There had to be a better way to manage than what I had learned in college and had experienced in the work place

I went looking for the answer, and while I didn't find it in one place, I found a piece here, and a piece there, and another piece over there. Then I put them together, and in 1993, I got my life back. American Retail Supply has since grown by leaps and bounds. I've started four other successful businesses since then. I love my job, and I love my life.

CHAPTER 5
Thanks Jeff

As I mentioned, I developed my management system in 1992. It allowed me to be Bobbie Radel's Dad, grow my original business many times, and start 4 more businesses. However, I didn't write this book until 2013. Here's what pushed me to write the book.

My son Travis and I lead a local group of business people in learning Dan Kennedy Marketing. I was facilitating a Mastermind Group of Kennedy Marketers at my house in the Seattle area when one of the members, Jeff Heiss, asked, "How did these local marketing groups get started?" I told Jeff that, among other things, I believed Dan Kennedy wants to leave a legacy of 'the millionaire maker' - a guy that helped hundreds, if not thousands, of people become millionaires by using his marketing ideas.

That led to a discussion of legacy. I said, "I don't have any desire to leave a legacy like Dan's. The only legacy I really care about is that when I pass, I want my family and close friends to say, 'I'm sure glad he was part of my life.'"

Jeff knew I had developed my management system that allowed me to be both Bobby Radel's Dad and a successful business owner. He replied, "But Keith, if you shared your management system with others, you could do that for other families."

It was getting close to Christmas with all of the thoughts about good will, family, the Christmas movies and all of those feelings. I prayed, and knew that it was time to bring my management system to market.

The Make-You-Happy Management System shows your team members (employees) that they are important, they make a difference, and they are truly the experts at what they do. When your team members know that you believe in them, they become better employees. They feel better about their jobs. They feel better about themselves and they go home to be better husbands, wives, and parents.

And, of course, the management system allows you to control your business and have the time and energy to be a better spouse, parent, grandparent, and friend.

CHAPTER 6
The 29-Year Search

If you've ever heard of TQM – Total Quality Management, I want you to know that my system is not TQM, but that's where it got its start.

In 1992, I attended a 3-day TQM Seminar sponsored by the Seattle Chamber of Commerce. The first speaker was about my age at the time and started by saying, "Until I found TQM I could have cared less if my business grew any more. It seemed like the only thing that grew as fast as my business were my headaches, and I sure as heck didn't want any more employees... talk about headaches."

Did I sit up and pay attention! That's exactly how I felt, and I was more than interested in hearing about this guy's management guru, Phil Crosby. I listened to the speaker and the rest of the presentations for 3 days and was absolutely jazzed to continue to learn and to get started with a management system that would work for me.

I read everything I could about Phil Crosby and while I liked some of his stuff, I didn't see how it could work for me. So I thought, *OK, I'll read TQM Guru #2, W. Edwards Deming and it will make sense.*

I was just more confused. Again, I liked some of Deming's ideas, but a lot of it was counter to Crosby, and the system as a whole just wouldn't work for me.

So I thought, *I'll read TQM Guru #3, Joseph Juran.* I figured he would put it all together and it would make sense. After reading Juran, I was only more confused. None of them had the answer. None had a complete management system that would get me excited about growing my business.

I was a B and C student all through grade school until I took psychology the first semester of my junior year in high school. I loved the instructor and I loved the subject. I finally figured out that I didn't need to be the class clown and that I could be smart. I aced the psychology class, and got straight A's the rest of the way through high school.

I went off to college not knowing what I wanted to do. I loved psychology but I didn't want to be a psychologist, psychiatrist, or social worker. The subject was really interesting but I knew I didn't want to work with messed up people all day, every day. I would have loved teaching, but frankly, I wanted to make more money. Math had always come easy for me, so I decided to major in math.

I became a math major and then took computer science. Back then, in computer programming, every line of code had to be entered onto a punch card. The simple programs we were running required 100 or more cards. If you made even one typing mistake, the program wouldn't run, and you had to go back to the beginning and check each digit... That drove me nuts! But that wasn't the worst of it. I also had to take Binary Logic, which was boring beyond belief. I then applied to the Business School and was accepted. I would use my math skills to become an accountant.

One of the requirements for the Business School was taking a marketing course. I soon realized that marketing was simply applied psychology. Holy cow! I could use the psychology I loved to do something I knew I would enjoy, and make a lot of money at the same time!

CHAPTER 7
You Can't "Dial-in" Quality

You're probably wondering what all this has to do with the management system I created? Deming, Juran, and Crosby were all manufacturing gurus. Deming, the "father" of TQM was a statistician in World War II. After the war he tried showing American manufacturers how to build quality products, but they weren't interested. There was so much demand for their products that it didn't matter if they made top quality products or not. Deming took his ideas to Japan – **Toyota Listened**.

As a statistician, everything for Deming was black and white, within tolerances or not (math). That works great in manufacturing where you can **dial-in** quality. You can build a better machine, with closer tolerances, and hire the best engineers to dial-in quality. But, in "people businesses" you can't dial-in quality.

I knew I couldn't just take Deming's methods and use them in a people business. I couldn't dial-in quality in a people business. **In people businesses, quality is meeting, and preferably exceeding, your customer's expectations every time, and the only way to get that is to get buy-in from your team.**

The secret was to use as much as I could from the TQM gurus of manufacturing, combine it with what I learned in business school and **Psychology**, and my years of experience working and managing, and create the Make-You-Happy Management System. The system is based on:

- Creating systems (written instructions) for everything you do.

- Replacing demotivating and counterproductive Performance Reviews with motivating, inspirational, and productive Personal Development Interviews.

- Installing a Customer Service System that creates happy customers who come back time and time again, and enthusiastically tell their friends about you.

- Getting **buy-in** from your team.

CHAPTER 8
The Power of Systems

You will take control of your business and your life when you create systems to run, control and improve your business with or without you there.

With the proper systems in place you will:

- Do the things you do in your business correctly, every time.
- Spend your time on the important things in your business and not on basic menial tasks.
- Have more time to spend on things **YOU WANT to do, not on things you have to do.**

I doubt this is the first time you've heard that systems are the key to controlling your business. The best-selling business book *The E-Myth Revisited*, by Michael Gerber is all about systems and Gerber has it exactly right. You need to **"let systems run the business and people run the systems" because "people come and go, but systems remain constant."**

Gerber's book is excellent, and I suggest you read it. With that said, there are some big problems with *The E-Myth Revisited*. I've met hundreds of business people who have read *The E-Myth Revisited*, but I don't know any who implemented what they learned from it to create all of the systems they needed to control their business. They don't create systems because they think systems take a tremendous amount of time to create, and they are complicated.

It's no wonder that's what they think. Here's how they describe a Business Management System at *emyth.com/business-coaching:*

It's a complex system of people and systems that are all evolving at the same time. To build a great business - to get out of survival mode - you need an outside perspective to help you see it clearly, someone who'll call it like it is and who won't waste your time and money with band-aids and tricks.

That is Complete Hogwash!

Sure, an effective business management system evolves, and you want to use advisors like your CPA, attorney and banker at times. However it is <u>not complex,</u> and you sure as heck don't need an outside perspective (nursemaid) other than your own employees (team) to implement an effective business management system into your business.

Ask yourself, why does a business coach want you to believe that an effective business management system is complex and that you need an outside perspective?

The answer is simple. If it's complex and you need an "outside perspective," then you need to hire them and pay hundreds, maybe thousands, of dollars each month... maybe forever.

Here's the Truth - Systems are Simple

My marketing mentor, Dan Kennedy, uses this example to show just how simple systems can be. When he uses valet parking at a particularly well-run business, he gets a business sized card from the valet. It is printed with the six things you should expect when you use the valet service. It's a very effective system that lets the customer know what to expect and tells the valet exactly what he or she should be doing. That's a system. Sure, some systems may need a longer explanation but everything you do in your business can be written into easy-to-understand instructions.

It's that simple. You create a System when you document - put in writing - something that needs to be done in your business.

You create an Effective Business Management System when you have everything you do documented, and when you have an Effective Performance Management System in place.

I know I've probably scared you off by mentioning Performance Management System, but let me assure you that I don't mean Performance Reviews because...

Performance Reviews Suck

I'll discuss how to replace de-motivating, demoralizing, and worst of all, counterproductive Performance Reviews with motivating Personal Development Interviews later on. First, let's see WHY you need systems (written documentation) for everything you do.

Here's why you need Systems.

When you hire someone, over time, the knowledge the person has about that job rises.

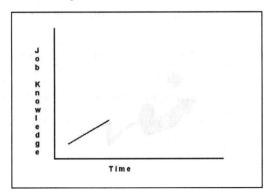

Without Systems (everything in writing), what happens when they leave?

The knowledge is gone and someone is back to training the new person one-on-one in everything that needs to be done.

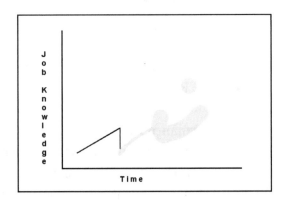

Over-time you're **lucky** if you make any progress. You hear it all of the time, "No one has ever been as good as Mary at that job."

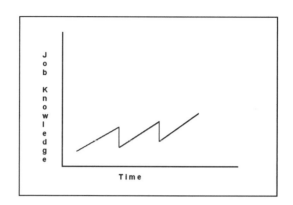

But what if you have systems? That is, written documentation for everything the person does in that position... What happens to knowledge when someone leaves and you have systems?

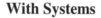

With Systems

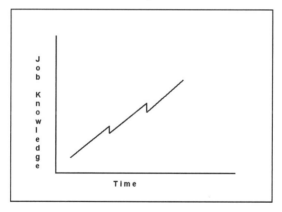

It's that simple. When they leave, and everything they do is documented, how hard is it to replace that person and get the new person up to speed? Just think of the amount of time you'll save.

My Friend and Mentor Dan Kennedy says, "All Wealth is Based on Systems"

When it's time to sell your business, what is it worth if you're critical to its success? Not much! What if you're not critical, and in fact, the business gets better whether you're there or not? What is your business worth now when it's time to sell? You know the answer.

When you get Buy-In from your team, have Systems in place for everything you do, use an effective Performance Feedback System, and use a proven Customer Service Training System to consistently deliver world class customer service, your business will improve whether you're there or not.

I Want to Make YOU Irrelevant

My goal for you, and all of my clients, is to make you irrelevant to the day-to-day, and then week-to-week, and then month-to-month operations of your business so you can create real wealth.

Earlier I told you about the 3-week Mediterranean cruise I went on and how I only told our operations manager what cruise line I was on, and the ship... that's it.

I knew I wasn't going to get a phone call. That's why I didn't need to worry about giving her any more information or getting an international phone number for 3 weeks. For the last 19 years, while on vacation, I've never gotten a phone call from work. That's the freedom you have when you have Systems in place.

But what was even better than no phone calls was that, when I got back, the business was running better than when I left.

CHAPTER 9
Improvement on Auto-Pilot

The business improves whether I'm there or not because that's what it does day in and day out, all of the time. We have Systems that guarantee it!

Everyone knows that his or her job is to do the task exactly as the System states, unless it doesn't take care of the customer. If it doesn't take care of the customer, they need to do what needs to be done to take care of the customer and then do what needs to be done to change the System. That means everyone is always looking to make things better.

No one in any of our businesses would ever say, "I didn't think it was my job," "I didn't think I should," or "I didn't think I could." Within two hours of starting their job, everyone understands that we hired both their brain and their body. This means they are expected to use both.

When you combine Systems like this, with Personal Development Interviews and Make-You-Happy Customer Service, your business will improve with or without you around, and that creates real wealth!

CHAPTER 10
Actions Speak Louder Than Words

When I introduced the new management system at a company-wide meeting in 1992, I told our team, "I know what you're thinking. You're thinking **this too will pass.** Keith has been to another seminar and got all jazzed up about this. I'll humor him and pretend it's the greatest thing since apple pie, but I know **this too will pass.** I want to tell you, this will not pass. This is how we will manage the business in the future and I think you'll be excited about it."

But I still had to back it up with actions

A number of years later the Make-You-Happy Management System led us to being named, **"The Best Small Business to Work for in Washington State"** by *Washington CEO Magazine.*

We didn't earn that honor because we had the highest pay, the greatest benefits, a child care center, foosball tables or any other bells and whistles. We earned it because Washington CEO Magazine determined that the management of our company, and our entire team, were committed to the same Belief, Vision, Mission and Goals.

Someone had nominated us as *The Best Business to Work For in Washington State.* I never found out who nominated us, but I decided to apply because the magazine promised to tell us how we did and why. I just wanted to know how we stacked up. I thought everyone here liked our Systems idea and thought the systems built a better business because they knew that we as a management team saw our team as experts at their jobs and that we truly valued and wanted their input to make the business better.

Washington CEO Magazine asked me to give them the names of three people they could interview in the company. Again, I hadn't entered the "contest" to win; I entered to find out how we were doing, so I sent them our entire employee (team member) list. The next thing I know they're calling me to do an interview because we were named the *"Best Small Business to Work for in Washington State."*

They told me we did a lot of things right, and the #1 reason we were named the best small business to work for is because our management philosophy, and company goals and objectives, could be verbalized, and were committed to, by our front line people better than any other entry. We were all on the same page. **We had BUY-IN.**

CHAPTER 11
How to Get BUY-IN

In that initial meeting, right after I told my team that "this will not pass," I showed them my management system. Here's how I explained it. This is a participative exercise, so work through it with me.

Answer the following question right here. Don't read any more until you answer this question. What are the 8 steps of solving a problem? Stop now and answer.

1.
2.
3.
4.
5.
6.
7.
8.

Now, assume you have the same question, "What are the 8 steps to solving a problem." But now you're part of a group with four other people and you have two guidelines:
1. Everybody must participate.
2. You need to achieve consensus with the answer.

Consensus means that you can all agree that you have a very good answer. You may not all agree with everything in the answer, but you accept it as a very good answer.

Also assume that one of the members of the group is trained to facilitate these meetings and get consensus; and the group is filled with people who work at solving problems for a living. The people you're working with know, from working experience, not theory, how to solve problems.

Now the question is, which of these scenarios gets a better answer to the question, "What are the 8 steps to solving a problem?" Is it by yourself, or in the group? When I do this exercise with groups, 95% of people say they get a better answer in the group.

Which takes longer? The group takes longer, of course. You need consensus in the group. That takes time. You can make your own list a lot quicker.

So, can we afford to do this with everything in our business? Absolutely not. But you'll want to use this type of system on the important things, the complicated things, and the things that affect more than one department in your business.

Why did I ask, "What are the 8 steps to solving a problem?" Because it's like many business decisions you need to make. There's no right answer. There's no wrong answer. There are some really bad answers. There are some really good answers. And there's everything in between.

Here's an example. Many years ago we purchased new computer software and we were supposed to be able to enter orders online while talking with the client. Months later, our staff was still writing orders by hand and entering them when they got off the phone. The software was fine if the customer didn't change their mind during the order, didn't order both a custom product and a stock product on the same order, or one of a dozen other scenarios. But for far too many orders, it was much easier to write the order down and then enter it in.

36

We decided to redesign the software from the ground up and to get the input we needed to make it truly client and user focused.

The sales people were involved during the entire process and we got accounting involved with issues like the customer being on a credit hold when they placed the order. When it came to processing non-stock orders we got purchasing involved. When it was time to address shipping issues we got the warehouse staff involved.

Management Types:
1. **X Theory** says, "I'm the owner, I'm the boss, I've built this company with my blood, sweat, and tears, so do what I say and don't ask any questions."
2. **Y Theory** is what I learned in college. It says, "I'm the owner, I'm the boss, I built this company with my blood, sweat, and tears. This is what I want you to do; tell me what you think, and I'll tell you whether it's ok or not."

At this point in the training, whether in person or on our DVD, I ask the employee, which would you rather work in? X or Y theory? Almost everyone answers Y. They want to have input.

I then ask, "Which get better answers to important issues, X or Y?" Everyone answers Y.

So virtually everyone would rather work in Y and almost everyone thinks you get better answers in Y theory.

But there's a third management type:

3. **Z Theory** says, "I'm the owner, I'm the boss, I'm the manager, I built this company with my blood, sweat, and tears. I know a lot, and when we have something that's important, I understand that my team knows a lot also. In fact, in regards to their job they likely know far more than I do. On those important decisions that involve others, I'm going to get stakeholders involved and find the best answer."

Again, at this point in the training we ask, which would you rather work in? Y or Z theory? Almost everyone answers Z. We then tell them if they would rather work in "X" or "Y," they might be in the wrong place because we hired both your body and your brain, and we want you to use both.

We then ask, "Which gets better answers, Y or Z?" Again, almost everyone answers Z.

Here's where real freedom comes for you. In the DVD and live training I then ask, "If we have a problem or an opportunity and we're an X theory management organization, whose problem is it?" The answer is: the boss' problem.

"If we're a Y theory management business, whose problem is it?" The boss' problem.

"If we have a problem or opportunity and we're a Z theory company, whose problem is it?" The answer, "Ours!"

With this we get, and we expect, everyone on the same side of the table working together to solve the problem. Once you create "buy-in" for this with your actions, you'll have real freedom, a business that gets better every day with or without you there, and the ability to go on vacation for 3 weeks and come back to a business running better than when you left.

You can't use Z Theory Management for everything. Your staff would spend all of their time in meetings. But the reality is, after it's been implemented for a while, not only will your business run much smoother and more efficiently, but you'll spend **far less time in meetings fixing things**.

The group of stakeholders (those who are affected by the problem or opportunity) that we get together to solve a problem or capitalize on an opportunity is called a Make-You-Happy Action Team. The result of their work is the written documentation (System) of how to do a particular job. We call this written documentation a Make-You-Happy Job Requirement.

When You Should Use Z Theory Management and Make-You-Happy Action Teams

- Whenever you're working on one of those big issues that will get a better answer when you get a group of stakeholders involved.
- When you have an issue that is causing conflict or problems in your business.
- When the results of what you decide will significantly affect another group. For example, if what the sales people decide is going to affect the warehouse, then we have at least one stakeholder from each group on the Make-You-Happy Action Team.
- When someone asks for one. For example, someone says, "I've tried to get this changed and I can't get it done. Can we get a group together and find the best way to do it?"

Continuous Improvement

It's critical that your team understands that you're relying on them to come up with small improvements in your business. You want them to understand that if you do 100 things 1% better, it will make a tremendous difference for your customers. You want them to understand that often, for the customer, it's the small things that matter.

Here's how I explain it in the DVD training for the Make-You-Happy Management System.

Let's assume you're going to buy a car, SUV, a mini-van, or whatever type of new vehicle you want. What is it that you're going to look for? What is important to you when looking for a new vehicle? I did this with a group of people, and this is what they came up with:

Price	Security System
Sunroof	Seat Belts
Ability to Tow	Kid Locks
CD Player	Automatic Transmission
AM/FM Radio	Reliability
DVD Player	4-Wheel Drive
Heated Seats	Airbags
Good Tires	Large Trunk
Nice Tires	Air Conditioning
Leather Interior	Power Locks
Good Financing	Automatic Windows
Good Gas Mileage	Automatic Doors
Status	Alarm System
Good Sales Rep	Silver Color
Cup Holders	GPS System
Anti-lock Brakes	

Now let's define a couple of terms. First, let's define a **Breakthrough**. A breakthrough is something that is big and probably costs a lot of money. It takes a lot of time, maybe a lot of research and development costs. It's a big deal. That's a breakthrough.

Let's define another term - **Continuous Improvement**. A continuous improvement is just what it sounds like - Better today than it was yesterday. Better this week than it was last week. Better this year than it was last year. Let's take a look at all of these things that people want when they get a new vehicle, and let's label them as breakthroughs or continuous improvements.

CI - Price	BT - Anti-Lock Brakes
CI - Sunroof	CI - Seat Belts
CI - Ability to Tow	BT - Good Gas Mileage and Power
CI - CD Player	BT - Automatic Transmission
CI - AM/FM Radio	CI - Reliability
CI - DVD Player	BT - 4-Wheel Drive
CI - Heated Seats	BT - Airbags
CI - Good Tires	CI - Large Trunk
CI - Nice Tires	CI - Air Conditioning
CI - Leather Interior	CI - Power Locks
CI - Good Financing	CI - Automatic Windows
CI - Security System	CI - GPS System
CI - Automatic Doors	CI - Kid Locks
CI - Status	CI - Alarm System
CI - Good Sales Rep	CI - Color
CI - Cup Holders	

Now let's go back and look at these. Price, sunroof, and ability to tow are obviously continuous improvements. The 4th, CD player, was a breakthrough when it was developed, but putting it in a vehicle was a continuous improvement. AM/FM radio and DVD player are like the CD player. Creating the product itself was a breakthrough, but putting it in a car was a continuous improvement. Going down the list we don't get to a breakthrough until we get to Anti-lock brakes.

Developing Anti-lock brakes was a breakthrough. I think Mercedes Benz was the first to develop anti-lock brakes. But how long did it take for the next company to copy anti-lock brakes? Maybe a year? How long to copy good gas mileage and power? Again, a year?

So while breakthroughs are very important, a lot of times they don't really make a huge difference. A lot of times they are easy to copy, or in the case of automobile safety, the government may require that the inventor sell the breakthrough to others.

Often what makes the difference to customers is the continuous improvement. That's what we want to be working on every day in our business. How can we be better this year than we were last year? How can we be better this week than we were last week? How can we be better today than we were yesterday? You want to improve 100 different things by 1% and when you do that you will be a truly <u>customer focused</u>, exceptional company.

The Make-You-Happy Management System can be summed up in one sentence.

**"Continuous improvement,
through empowered work groups and individuals."**

That's what you want to achieve. Make sure that every team member understands that you didn't just hire their body. You hired their brain also, and you want them to be thinking, each and every day, "How can we do things better in our business?" Be sure they understand that they are important; they are the key to providing Make-You-Happy Customer Service that creates happy customers who come back time after time and enthusiastically tell others.

Creating Systems

As I said earlier, Systems are not complex. Here are a few examples of Make-You-Happy Job Requirements (Systems) that apply to everyone in our company.

Make-You-Happy Job Requirement

MJR-ALL-26: Fundraisers
Position: All
Created: February 22, 2000

You are welcome to bring your fundraisers to work, and advertise and display them using the following guidelines:

Advertising
• You may use your E-mail to announce the product. For example: My son Joey's fundraiser for his baseball team is in the lunchroom. Good Candy!
• You may use voicemail.
• You may put a note in everyone's bin.
• You may display the product in the lunchroom with a small sign.

No-No's
- Nothing other than ARS products are to be displayed in the showroom. An ARS product is a product ARS sells to make a profit. The VP of marketing is responsible for showroom display.
- Do not approach anyone directly with requests for donations.

When someone starts here at American Retail Supply they are asked to read the Make-You-Happy Job Requirements that apply to their job and to everyone in the company. They may not remember the details of this MJR when they want to bring their kid's fundraiser to work, but they'll likely remember that it was addressed in a MJR, find and read it; or ask their manager about it.

At worst, if someone brings a fundraiser to work and approaches others, they are simply reminded of the MJR. We created that Make-You-Happy Job Requirement on February 22nd, 2000 and we've never had to address the issue again.

Here's another MJR that applies to everyone. This assures that the building is secured properly every night.

Make-You-Happy Job Requirement

MJR-ALL-03: Last Person in the Building
Position: All
Created: May 15th, 1991
Revised: January 17th, 2012

It is the responsibility of the last person leaving the building each day to make sure that everything is secure. The last person in the building must:

- Make sure that you really are the last person in the building by physically walking around, looking around, and calling out if anyone is still in the building.
- Make sure all of the doors in the office and warehouse areas are locked.
- Turn out all of the lights.
- Make sure the coffee pot in the lunch room is turned off.
- Set the Security System
- Lock both the top and bottom locks of the door when you leave.

Here's an MJR that applies to the Accounting Department to ensure that we are consistent with depreciation, amortizing or expensing items.

Make-You-Happy Job Requirement

MJR-ACC-05: Depreciation and Amortization
Position: Accounting
Created: June 11th, 2007

Use this guideline to determine if something purchased is depreciated as an asset or expensed.

If the item has a useful life of more than one year and costs more than $500, it should be considered an asset and classified to one of the accounts in the 1700 series so it can be depreciated over its useful life.

All items that cost less than $500 should be expensed.

Items that cost more than $500 with a useful life of less than one year should also be expensed.

As you can see, systems are not complicated!

In fact you could likely use all of the MJRs above, as is, or tweaked a bit in your business. The Make-You-Happy Management System I developed for businesses like yours includes 456 Make-You-Happy Job Requirements that you can use as is, or tweak a bit to use in your business.

In the system, we provide clients with green, yellow and red sticky tabs. You simply thumb through the binder of Make-You-Happy Job Requirements and put a green sticky pad on MJRs you can use, as is, with no changes. Put a yellow tab on MJRs that you can use with some changes. Put a red tab on MJRs to which you need to change significantly to work in your business. Don't put a tab on MJRs that you can't use. Implement the MJRs with green tabs immediately, tweak the yellow tabbed MJRs, and you are on your way to a systemized business and FREEDOM!

CHAPTER 12
Turn Your Team into a System Creating Machine

You personally should start the process described in the previous chapter and then turn it over to managers or other team members. This is huge in terms of empowering your team and getting them to understand that you hired not only their body, but also their brain. They'll know you truly understand that they are the experts and you need them involved.

It also, of course, means you don't need to do all of the work. **The Make-You-Happy Management System is all about making less work for you – not more.**

Picture this

You've watched the DVD in the Make-You-Happy Management System that discusses X, Y, and Z theories of management. The DVD tells every team member that they are important, that you need their help and input to build a good stable business, that you hired both their body and their brain, and that together you will be creating MJRs for everything you do.

Now you scan through the 32 Make-You-Happy Job Requirements included in the Make-You-Happy Management System for the Receptionist and find two you think are very close to what you do in your business. You tweak them to what you think you currently do.

Critical Empowerment Strategy

Now you'll meet with the receptionist and tell her that you wrote up these two MJRs as you **think** they should be done, and ask her to change them as needed for our business. **With this you will have reinforced the process of recognizing your team as experts and empowering them.**

Now it's time to show everyone all of the MJRs in the system that apply to their specific jobs, ask them to see which ones can apply to your business, have them tab them with green, yellow, or red sticky tabs, and then edit them as needed. Ask them to complete one a day, one every other day, or one a week; whichever is appropriate for your business.

Do this with your entire team and before you know it you'll have scores of systems (MJRs) and you'll start getting the huge benefits of having systems and an empowered team.

The first problem I discussed with the concepts in The E-Myth is the idea that systems are complex and you need an "outside perspective." They're not! You and your team can do it.

But there's another problem with Gerber's concepts in the E-Myth. Gerber calls his system *"the franchise model."* In his model you create all of the Systems and give them to your employees.

That means that all of your business improvement is dependent on you, and I hate to break this to you, but you just ain't that smart.

But You AND Your Team Are That Smart!

The franchise model works fine if you're McDonald's and you have a bunch of people dedicated to creating all of those

Systems, and testing this verses that, but you don't have that luxury.

In the Make-You-Happy Management System your team, and you, are the experts. There is no question that the guys in my warehouse know more about what works in the warehouse than I do. The ladies in purchasing know their problems and issues better than I do. And there is no question that my combined team is a whole lot smarter than I am.

When your entire team knows that you value their input, expect their help to make things better every day, and you get their input on the big issues we discussed earlier you'll truly control your business and your life.

We initially implemented the Make-You-Happy Management System in American Retail Supply (ARS), a wholesale distribution business. When it worked at American Retail we implemented it at Superior Display, a manufacturing business I own... and Ureka! We found that even though the two businesses operate independent of each other, most of the MJRs transferred from one business to the other with little, or no, changes. Now we use the Make-You-Happy Job Requirements as the basis for every system in all of our businesses.

CHAPTER 13
Continually Improve

This is Critical; the bottom of each MJR has this printed on it:

"This Make-You-Happy Job Requirement is designed to insure we meet or exceed our internal and external customer expectations. Perform exactly like the requirement unless you find it does not meet or exceed those expectations. If you find it no longer meets or exceeds expectations, take care of the customer. Then, you are responsible for helping to change it to what we and our customers need."

This insures that your business continually improves.

You may have noticed the terms: internal customer and external customer. External customers are customers. The people who pay you money for what you do.

In the Make-You-Happy Management System, we make sure that everyone knows that they also have internal customers. Internal customers are the people you work with. They're your vendors, suppliers, the mail-man, and of course, your co-workers.

**Anyone who is dependent upon
the quality of your work is your Internal Customer**

Here's the idea. Our sales rep is on the phone with a customer taking an order. Now obviously when they're on the phone taking an order, the customer is 'the customer.' But when they hang up the phone, who is 'the customer' now? The

51

customer now is the person in the warehouse who's going to pull the order.

If the order is not entered properly, the warehouse person can't do their job. If the rep entering the order messes up, the warehouse person will take more time than necessary, or they're not going to be able to fill the order properly. So, as soon as the sales rep hits 'process' on the order, the customer is the warehouse person. The rep needs to make sure to take care of the internal customer as well as they took care of the customer placing the order.

The warehouse person who pulls the order takes the packing list off the printer and pulls the order. Who is the customer for the person who pulled the order?

The customer now is the person who packages it and gets it ready to ship. If the order puller doesn't pull the order properly, the guy who packages it is going to ship it incorrectly or he's going to hold everything up, then stop and go pull it properly.

Once the order is packaged, who is the customer? In our case, it's the FedEx guy. If our packager hasn't packaged it properly then the FedEx guy can't get it to our customer properly and we mess up the customer.

So this idea of the internal customer is incredibly important. But that doesn't mean we need to be as 'peaches and cream' when we're dealing with our internal customers as much as we are with external customers. You can be yourself a little more, but you still need to give internal customer service that's exceptional.

Back to the statement that is at the bottom of each MJR. "This Make-You-Happy Job Requirement is designed to insure we meet or exceed our internal and external customer expectations. Perform exactly like the requirement unless you find it does not meet or exceed those expectations. If you find it no longer meets or exceeds expectations, take care of the customer. Then, you are responsible for helping to change it to what we and our customers need."

So, everyone understands that if a MJR does not take care of internal and external customers, it is their responsibility to take care of the customer and then to help change the MJR so it does take care of the customer.

When this is implemented in your business you'll never again hear, "I didn't think I could..." or "I didn't think I should..." or any excuse for not using their brain.

CHAPTER 14
Performance Reviews Suck!

This chapter should have been titled Performance Management. I didn't title it that because most people think that the only type of performance management is performance reviews and everyone knows that performance reviews suck.

Shortly after developing my Make-You-Happy Management system for other businesses, we had a friend over for dinner. My wife had told her that I had been in Florida and Michigan giving presentations on my management system, so she said, "Tell me about this management stuff you're doing."

She was retired from a large aerospace company in the Puget Sound area and I knew she had never been in management. So rather than talk about systems, management theory and all of the problems managers face; I took another approach.

I said, "When you were at B***** you had performance reviews, right?"

She rolled her eyes and said, "Yes."

I asked, "What did you think of them?"

She replied, "They Sucked!"

You need to understand that Mary is one of those people who wouldn't say sh** if she had a mouthful, so I knew I had the title for this section of the book, "Performance Reviews Suck."

I speak to a lot of groups and I often ask how many of the people in the room have been on the giving or receiving end of a performance review. Most of the people in the room raise their hand. Then I ask, "How many of you like performance reviews, think they are motivating, and lead to the results that the organization wants?" Once in a while, a hand or two will go up, but most often, no one raises their hand.

In this chapter I'll tell you why performance reviews not only suck, but are counterproductive. I'll also introduce you to Personal Development Interviews (PDIs).

Going back to my conversation with Mary, I told her a little about PDIs and said, "Just listening to what they're called, a Performance Review, or a Personal Development Interview; which would you rather have?"

Her reply: "A Personal Development Interview."

If you've ever been on the giving or receiving end of a performance review then you know they suck. Everyone hates them; they're de-motivational, discouraging and most importantly... they don't lead to the behavior you want.

Performance Reviews are like trying to drive your car by looking in the rearview mirror.

Performance Reviews are like trying to drive your car by looking in the rearview mirror.

As a parent of a teenager, can you imagine getting the performance you want from your kid by having an annual performance review? Would every six months work? How about quarterly? Your employees can not be scarier than a teenager.

Your employees can't be scarier than a teenager!

In 1993, when I created my management system, I took control of my business and my life... but I knew there was something missing.

The system set expectations for exactly what needed to be done, but in regards to Performance Management we were still doing Performance Reviews. While trying to put on my "best face" for our team in regards to performance reviews, the truth is I hated them. I knew they were de-motivating, and finally determined that they were actually counterproductive and stopped doing them.

I met Vince Zirpoli in 2005 and knew immediately that I found the missing link. My management system was now complete with a Performance Management System that actually worked. I was now ready to answer the pleas from my business owner friends and create my management system for others.

CHAPTER 15
Effective Performance Management

In this chapter we'll discuss how to replace de-motivating, discouraging and counterproductive performance reviews with motivating, inspiring and most importantly PRODUCTIVE Personal Development Interviews.

When employed properly, an effective performance management system permeates the organization with a philosophy of catching people doing things right. Most businesses focus on catching people doing things wrong.

Catching people doing things wrong is called management by exception. When businesses utilize management by exception, they're watching for people to do things incorrectly. As a result, they stymie creativity in the organization. If every time I do something wrong and the boss catches me, but he doesn't catch me when I'm doing the right things, then I fail to take steps out in front and really help the organization grow by using my creativity.

Conversely, when we start catching people doing things right, we encourage empowerment. People start to do things in the organization. Productivity improves on an ongoing basis. So, the whole organization doesn't just come from management, but employees and management are interacting with each other. People are picking each other up. The organization is permeated with a motivating environment.

The second benefit that comes as a result of an effective performance management system is that you create a learning organization. Researchers tell us that as we move forward, people are going to stay with organizations where they have an opportunity to grow and learn. There are going to be many more skilled positions than there are people to fill them. And if there are a lot of skilled positions and not enough people to fill them, money isn't going to make the difference. Money is going to be a given. You're going to have to pay in the competitive market to get good people. But they want to work in a place where they can grow, where they can enjoy themselves, where they can use their creativity to help the organization grow, and that happens in a learning organization.

Before we discuss Personal Development Interviews in depth, it's important to understand a couple of other concepts. The first is that in all organizations, systems have at a minimum influence and a maximum control over the behavior of individuals. It's critical to understand this because if you don't, you'll take a band-aid approach to correcting situations rather than finding what system is controlling the behavior and then changing it.

The problem with this is that far too often the "systems" are not really the best way to do things, but have simply been handed down from one person to the next. Have you ever played "The Whisper Game?"

One person starts by whispering a secret at one end of the group, and the secret is whispered from person to person until it goes around the entire group. It's amazing how the original message has changed by the time it gets all the way around. Now imagine if that message was the wrong message in the first place. In other words, on the job, that particular duty was not done correctly in the first place.

You Must Manage The 95-percentors

The second concept is the 5-percenter. If you look at any organization, you'll find about 5% of the people are self-starters. They are self-motivated. They join the organization and management says "Go in that direction," and they go in that direction. They plan, they organize, they motivate themselves, they control their activities, and they go in that direction. They do a super job.

The 5-percenter is often selected to move into management. You are likely a 5-percenter.

When 5-percenters move into management they're told they have to coach, motivate, train and develop people; and their automatic response is... "No one had to watch me. No one had to tell me how to do it. I just did it."

They don't understand that they are managing 95-percenters. The 95-percenters are good people, but they need coaching, leadership, development, and follow-through. The key is that the manager has to understand this, and understand that he is more than a manager, or a director. The manager needs to be a trainer, coach, facilitator, developer, motivator, counselor, and administrator.

With that said, it's critical to understand that all development is self-development. You cannot develop another person. You cannot motivate another person. You can create an environment in which they motivate themselves and you facilitate their development, and as you facilitate their development you have to know that you cannot be the know-it-all guru. Managers who believe they have to be the know-it-all guru do not develop people.

You want your team to use their creativity. You want to empower them. You want them to come up with ideas. You teach them the process that leads to the objectives you want. Once they've proved to you that they can get the results, it's time to turn the process over to them.

You may be like a lot of business owners who were 5-percentors. Because of your work ethic and knowledge you became dissatisfied working for a large organization and decided to start your own business.

Many business owners are very successful entrepreneurs until the management systems they learned at their old job catch up to them and create similar frustrations in their own business... But now, it all comes down on you.

What is an effective feedback system?

Each person needs to have **goals/objectives**. There have to be **strategies and tactics** that are going to be employed to bring those goals and objectives to fruition. The manager has to receive **continuous feedback** letting him know what kind of progress is being made. And, there has to be an **adjustment** when you see the individual is not making progress - adjustment and corrective action that gets the individual back on target.

It's a complete system. You use this type of system every day. When you drive to a morning meeting you use this system. You set a goal of getting to the meeting on time. You develop strategies and tactics. You get to bed on time. You set your alarm to be ready to leave by a certain time. You determined the route. You get feedback from your speedometer, your odometer, and your watch. If you think you're going to be late, you step on the accelerator to get back on target. That is an effective performance feedback system, and we all utilize it every day. When we don't employ it completely, we do not have an effective system, and then we're subject to the environment as to whether we achieve our goals.

Every member of your team needs to have goals, with effective feedback, and there has to be an adjustment and corrective action taken along the way.

Think of it this way. Let's assume that you are driving an automobile, and that you want to be 50 miles down the road in one hour. It's important that you be there at a specific time, and you cannot go above the 55 mile an hour speed limit. There are no other detriments. All you have to do is drive. Your automobile is mechanically sound. You get in the automobile, and you start to drive. You can do that. It's easy right? All you have to do is average between 50 and 55 miles an hour and you'll be there on time.

Now let's assume that before you start the trip someone gets in the automobile, takes out the speedometer, the odometer, and you don't have a watch. They remove the radio, and take down all the signs along the way. They've taken away your feedback system. Now how do you feel? Do you feel the anxiety and frustration? Do you feel the frustration your team feels when you say, "Go get those goals," but with no supporting system in place to make sure they're getting the feedback and taking the necessary corrective action to get there? In order to be effective, every team member has to have individual objectives with effective continuous feedback.

Here's how lots of businesses develop. The entrepreneur, who is of course a 5-percenter, becomes unhappy working for a big organization. So he starts his own businesses, and he works all kinds of hours. Time means nothing to him. He wants to succeed. If he could work 50 hours a day, he would work 50 hours a day to bring his goal to fruition.

Initially, he surrounds himself with like-minded people. People who buy into his vision, who agree they can make something out of this company, and who work very hard. After a period of time, without realizing it, they start to put on the 95-percenters.

Managers often say, "I'm going to only hire 5-percenters." But, regardless of how you test, you can't tell who is a 5-percenter when you interview him,. The testing only tells you their aptitude. It doesn't tell you whether they're going to do it. It tells you whether they have the ability to do it.

The owner doesn't realize what he's putting on 95-percenters because if I sit down with anyone and say, "Tell me about yourself" - what do you think they are going to tell you? They are going to say, "Hey, man, I can do a good job. I really get out there. I work hard. I solve problems." They are going to tell you everything you want to hear. They know how to sell you, and they are going to sell you on themselves. The entrepreneur doesn't realize it and he continues to put on the 95-percenters and problems mount.

Again, the 95-percenters are good people, but they need management. They need coaching. They need help.

The business owner begins to see
- Shrinking margins
- Plateauing or falling sales
- High turnover
- Poor morale
- Poor quality or high error rate

64

- Declining market share
- Resistance to change.

What does the entrepreneur do when he sees these problems? Initially he puts a band-aid approach on it. Morale's low. Let's have a party. So we have a party. Everybody's happy. Have a few drinks. And it may alleviate the problem for a short period of time, but not long after that the problems are back again.

Or let's give everybody a raise or a bonus, which does help for a short period of time, but the problem comes back because the problem that you see is not the actual problem. It's a symptom of an ineffective performance management system. These are symptoms from problems and not the real problems because if an effective performance management system is in place, these problems are minimized or eliminated. But, by addressing the symptoms, they only postpone the inevitable.

So, the entrepreneur has 1 of 4 choices:

1. If margins shrink too much, he goes out of business. If you're not making money, there's no point in staying in business.

2. In lots of organizations, the manager loves the business, and he shrinks it. It becomes a small business where they all work a hundred hours a week. He works very hard, but he has complete control. It's a centralized organization where the owner is wearing many hats. He's the marketer. He's the accountant. He does a number of things. But he stays in business.

3. Lots of managers don't want to make the change. They don't want to have to do what they have to do to change their

65

organization and to functionalize it to become a growing organization. So, figuring they have all the systems in place, they sell it to a larger company.

4. He changes his system of management. The system of management with centralized control is no longer applicable. People have to be empowered. Delegation has to take place within the organization, and he or she has to take a systemic approach to it. There has to be a system in place that challenges everyone, develops everyone, and focuses on the goals that you are trying to achieve in the leadership of the company.

An Effective Performance Management System has 7 components and if you understand these components and employ them, you can't fail:

1. Personal Development Interview
2. Objectives
3. Objective Focused Activities
4. Feedback
5. Measurement
6. Reinforcement
7. Coaching

1. Personal Development Interview

The Personal Development Interview (PDI) is the power source of an Effective Performance Management System. PDI's will need to be regularly scheduled and held weekly, every other week, or at the very least, monthly.

In areas where you want to see a lot of change, a lot of improvement, have a lot of opportunity, or have challenges; you'll have them more often. In other areas that are very much under control you'll have them less often. Typically the lower the job function, the shorter the meeting.

Initially, don't expect to be an expert at PDIs. You have to work at it on a continuous basis. So often people expect change to happen overnight - it doesn't. We change in tiny increments, and that's one of the purposes of the Personal Development Interview.

The PDI is where you'll catch people doing things right. Your job is to pick them up, keep them excited about their job, and discuss corrective action. When you're discussing corrective action it's critical that you frame it properly. When you frame it properly and sandwich the corrective action between positive reinforcement and catching them doing things right, you'll see improvement that you never dreamed possible.

But how much time does all this take?

When I talk with business owners about Personal Development Interviews, the first question is, "Who has the time for that?"

Here are the facts: I own five businesses and conduct PDI's with the six people who report directly to me. I meet with each person, every other week, for about 20 minutes. So, on average, I spend one hour a week in PDIs. That means, because of the systems we have in place, I spend one hour per week managing five businesses. I spend the rest of my time working on the important things that grow my businesses, and the things I (enjoy) want to work on.

Research has shown that the average executive interacts with subordinates at least 37 times per week. Two, three, five minutes at a time. What if you and your subordinate got into the habit of discussing only critical issues right away and left the others for your regularly scheduled PDI? You will find that PDI's actually free up time for you, your managers, and your entire team.

Personal Development Interviews

As I mentioned before, for the most part you don't want to be the know-it-all guru during PDI's. No doubt, there are times when you have to be the know-it-all. For instance when you're working with a brand new person, and they don't know the processes. But, shortly after that, it turns into a meeting in which you're eliciting ideas from them. You're priming the pump to help them. Each week, when they realize that you're giving their ideas consideration they'll get better at it.

When that interview is running properly, the interviewer (you or your managers) will be talking about 20% of the time and the subordinate will be talking 80% or more. Sometimes the manager only talks 5%, but these managers know what questions to ask, and they're guiding the individual. They're facilitating growth.

Let's assume you, or a manager, are having a PDI and the subordinate comes up with an idea you don't like. You need to "frame" your response. If your response is, "That won't work" they're going to close their mind. What if you responded with, "Well, you know, that could possibly work, but what will you do if...", and then introduce the reason why you know it won't work.

Maybe they have thought about your objection and found a way around it. Now two people have grown. If they haven't found a way around it, then they'll come back with, "Yeah, I hadn't thought of that, okay." Now it's time for the manager to ask, "How do you think you'll solve that problem?" The responsibility for finding solutions lies with the interviewee, not the interviewer. This is the way people grow in the organization.

Another key to effective PDI's is that the person being interviewed should leave pumped up, ready to go after every interview. Your job, as the interviewer, is to make sure they are pumped up, ready to go, and achieve their objectives. The only time they should leave a Personal Development Interview disappointed is when you're ready to fire them.

I need to tell you I didn't believe that at first. I couldn't understand how you could get the behavior you want without constructive criticism, but when I practiced what I learned from Vince I was blown away, and that's why I teamed with Vince Zirpoli to add Personal Development Interview training to my management system.

The reality is, if you can send them out of that meeting feeling good about themselves - not falsely, but because they achieve something, then they learned something new and made progress toward their goals. This means you're moving in the right direction.

2. Objectives

Everyone in the organization must have objectives - specific objectives - and those objectives have to relate to where you're going as an organization. If they don't relate, either directly or indirectly to where we're going as an organization, then you have to question, "Do we need that position?" If they relate to where you're going, then you're going to make progress. But you cannot manage objectives. You can only measure objective focused activities. This is critical so I'll repeat it:

You cannot manage objectives.
You can only measure <u>objective focused activities</u>.

3. Objective Focused Activities – The Missing Link

You **can** manage the activity in which someone engages. When they say they're going to finish a project according to schedule, that's an activity. At the end of the first week, you want to know where they are on that. How are they doing? Are they on schedule? You can't wait until the project is supposed to be completed, and then find out. Again, this is like driving your car by looking through the rearview mirror. It's too late.

4. Feedback

Without adequate feedback, you're managing by circumstance. You're putting out fires. You're not managing by design. When you're getting feedback, you're reading it and taking the necessary corrective action.

This is very much like that trip you want to take 50 miles down the road, but you don't have a speedometer and just hope you get there on time and don't get a ticket. You'd never consider that.

Think of how many times you look down at the speedometer and take corrective action, maybe 2 or 3 times each mile. What's so different about the organization? You need timely feedback in order to coach, facilitate, and lead people.

You and your managers give and get feedback on Objective Focused Activities during your Personal Development Interviews.

5. Measurement

When you look at the statistics, trends, and measurable deficiencies, you're in a position to take corrective action, not based on subjective thoughts, but on actual facts that you can share with the individual. When they see the objectivity of it, they accept it.

You can't just measure the end result. You need to measure the activities leading to that end result also. You need to measure to identify strengths and weaknesses. You can then find out where problems are and address them.

As managers we must set the priorities. People respond to the areas where their supervisors show concern, but that concern has to be continuous. It can't be sporadic. You can't sit down and say, "You're doing a terrible job in this area here," and then talk to them a month later about it.

When there are issues you need to address, it's important to bring them up in the right manner. You can say to a girl, "When I look at you time stands still" or "You have a face that would stop a clock." One of these gets the results you want and one gets you punched. You can bring things out in a negative manner that creates push back or in a manner that makes progress.

6. Reinforcement

This is creating the motivating environment during the personal development interview by catching people doing things right.

Here's one example of how reinforcing properly works miracles.

When you're sitting down in an interview with someone, and you say, "Ben, tell me how you did that. You did a good job; tell me how you did it." Ben wasn't watching himself do it. So, he gives you a combination, unconsciously, of what he perceived himself doing, and he kind of mingles it in with what he thinks you want to hear.

That's good. That is not bad. It's good because now the words come out of Ben's mouth. Ben's behavior begins to change in order to conform to the words that come out of his mouth. With the exception of a brand new person, They bring what they should be doing up to a conscious level and walk out the meeting saying, "That sounded pretty good. I think that's the way I'll do it."

That's the way behavior changes, and it changes in almost insignificant increments from week to week. You can't see it, but if you take a look from January to June, substantial behavior change takes place. The behavior change slows down if you do it every other week. The more behavior change you want, or the more opportunities to improve, the more often you conduct your PDIs.

7. Coaching

The manager has many roles. Sure you're a director, but you're also a leader, coach, counselor, motivator, trainer, administrator, and many more beyond that. In addition, whether you like it or not, the performance of individuals is often affected by domestic problems and you may need to help individuals get through them.   We'll talk about this more under situational leadership.

This picture shows the wrong way to conduct a personal development interview.

This is the wrong way to conduct a personal development interview.

You don't want to sit on the other side of the desk when you conduct your PDIs.   Sitting on the other side of the desk portrays authority.   I'm the boss.   You're the subordinate. Generally the best way to hold the interview is by having the employee sit on the same side of the desk as you.   You don't want to portray authority.   You're a coach.   You're a guide. You're a motivator. You want to help them grow and develop.

This is the right way to conduct a personal development interview.

You want to literally and figuratively be on the same side of the table working together.

CHAPTER 16
Just Another "Feel-Good" Buzzword?

I'm mostly a black and white kind of guy. There's good, there's bad. There's right, there's wrong. There's proper behavior, there's stupid behavior. You succeed, or you fail; and you don't blame anyone else.

So when I heard the term "Situational Leadership" I thought, *Holy cow, another feel good, politically correct excuse for not performing.* I was wrong – way wrong.

Situational Leadership

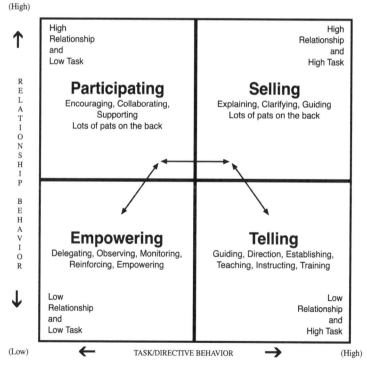

(High)

R
E
L
A
T
I
O
N
S
H
I
P

B
E
H
A
V
I
O
R

High
Relationship
and
Low Task

Participating
Encouraging, Collaborating,
Supporting
Lots of pats on the back

High
Relationship
and
High Task

Selling
Explaining, Clarifying, Guiding
Lots of pats on the back

Empowering
Delegating, Observing, Monitoring,
Reinforcing, Empowering

Telling
Guiding, Direction, Establishing,
Teaching, Instructing, Training

Low
Relationship
and
Low Task

Low
Relationship
and
High Task

(Low)   ←   TASK/DIRECTIVE BEHAVIOR   →   (High)

Situational Relationship Behavior is the extent to which the leader engages in 2-way communication; in other words, your interaction with people.

High relationship means you're highly engaged. You're giving them additional training and support on an ongoing basis. You're interacting with them quite frequently.

Low relationship behavior means that you're not as engaged in 2-way communication.

Task Behavior is the extent to which the leader is engaged in spelling out the duties and responsibilities. High task behavior means the manager is more detailed and directive toward telling the subordinate step-by-step what to do.

Low task behavior is when the manager assigns the task, delegates the task, and is not involved with actually getting the job done.

A new employee (team member) typically starts in Q1 and the manager does a lot of **Telling** (high task, low relationship). There is a lot of instruction showing them how to do the job. You're not patting them on the back yet because they haven't shown anything yet. You're teaching and training them, so there is not a lot of relationship behavior.

After a few months the new employee is making some progress and it's time to move from telling to **Selling** (high task, high relationship). The manager is still directing and showing, but the communication is more 2-way. The manager gives a lot of reinforcement while explaining, clarifying and persuading. The manager is mining for ideas from the team member and teaching them to think on their own. The leader still defines the roles and tasks, but seeks ideas and suggestions. The leader pats them on the back. The more you can guide them to thinking things out the more beneficial it is to you in the future.

As the individual grows, it's time for the manager to move from selling to **Participating** (high relationship, low task). The person understands the job and knows how to do it, but doesn't have a lot of confidence yet. They need reinforcement on an ongoing basis until they develop confidence. The manager gives the individual a lot of support, pats him on the back, and stays very close. Because the individual knows the job, there is much less directive behavior from the manager.

As the team member becomes more and more competent, he becomes a true expert at the job and the manager moves to **Empowering** (low relationship, low task). The team member is doing 80% or more of the talking during the PDI with the manager. The manager is observing, monitoring, reinforcing, and delegating.

Your goal as the manager is to get your staff to Quadrant 4, but as the graph above shows, it's not a one way street. Depending on the job or task, you may move down or up a quadrant, or even two – and sometimes even three. In one of my businesses, one of my vice presidents is fabulous at her job and my management style is almost always empowering. But she's not a numbers person, so when it comes to working with numbers my management style moves to Participating and sometimes to Selling or even Telling.

It's also important to understand that you're working with people, not machines. We all have personal lives away from business and for all of us, <u>even us 5-percentors</u>, our personal lives influence us at work. Sometimes it's critically important to move down a quadrant when a team member has personal problems. Leaving your empathy and understanding behind, you have a lot invested in someone who's in Q4. Moving up on the relationship scale to Participating or even to Selling is sometimes critical to get that person back up to speed. And, of course, if things get worse you may need to move to Telling.

Implementing Personal Development Interviews in Your Business

Here are the five components you'll need for each position in your business in order to conduct effective personal development interviews:

Job Description
Objectives
Reportable Objectives
Activity Log
Interview Guide

We call these five components JORIAs. Some components of the JORIA are ever changing, and some are much more stagnant. Once you have a great Job Description then it likely won't change much, but you'll certainly want to add, subtract, and edit it to some degree. The same goes for Objectives - you might add and subtract some, but not a lot.

Reportable Objectives, the Activity Log, and the Interview Guide should always be changing and evolving. As a reportable objective becomes routine for the person accomplishing it, you don't need to take time in your PDI to discuss it. It's time for that reportable objective to be relegated to an "Objective."

78

Here's an example of an objective that was reportable during PDI's, but is now relegated to an objective. This is in regards to providing Point-of-Sales computers to retailers. "Contact all new clients within two days after the arrival of the system and continue contacts on a systematic basis." We don't discuss this during our PDIs any longer because it is always accomplished. It has become routine. It is still included as an objective, but it is not something we discuss in PDIs.

Here's another example. A number of years ago we had an objective of shipping every order received by noon on the same day the order was received. FedEx comes every day at 4 P.M. We decided we wanted to do better, so we created an objective of, "If the product is in stock, ship every order placed by 3:30 P.M. on the same day we receive the order." That became a reportable objective backed up by a time stamp on the order when it was placed and a time stamp when it was shipped. We were able to track our progress towards the goal. After a while, meeting the goal was routine. We do it every day. That objective is still an objective. We don't want to lose sight of it. But it's not a reportable objective that gets discussed in a PDI.

Combine this with Make-You-Happy Job Requirements, employee empowerment and Make-You-Happy Customer Service that we'll discuss later, and continual improvement becomes routine in your business.

Creating JORIAs

The best way to show you how to create and use JORIAs in your business is to give you an example. Here is the JORIA for the sales manager of one of our businesses.

Job Description – The Job Description includes the job title, who the position reports to, what job positions report to this person, a summary of the position and the essential duties and responsibilities. To ensure that everyone knows what's expected, it is critical to have detailed duties and responsibilities. A great job description makes hiring the right person easier as well.

Notice that the first essential duty and responsibility for the Vice President of Sales is, "So that our business continually improves and we meet or exceed our internal and external customer expectations, execute every Make-You-Happy Job Requirements exactly as written unless you find it does not meet or exceed expectations. If you find it no longer meets or exceeds expectations, take care of the customer. Then, take responsibility to change the MJR to what we and our customers need."

This is the first duty and responsibility for every position in the company. This reinforces the value of MJRs in our business, insures we continually improve and document the improvement in our MJRs, and that every individual understands that it is their job to help continually improve the business.

As you'll see in the examples below, this emphasis on continual improvement and identifying deficiencies is reinforced in the objectives, reportable objectives, activity log and interview guide.

American Retail Supply
Job Description

Job Title: Vice President Sales
Reports To: President
Supervises: 10 Sales People,   1 Sales Assistant,

1 Receptionist, 1, Catalog Coordinator, 1 Web Coordinator

SUMMARY

Responsible for the development of strategic goals and objectives for the American Retail Supply Sales Department. Also plans, organizes, coordinates and directs the activities of reporting personnel toward the achievement of such goals and objectives by performing the following duties personally or through subordinates.

ESSENTIAL DUTIES AND RESPONSIBILITIES include the following. Other duties may be assigned.

1. So that our business continually improves and we meet or exceed our internal and external customer expectations, execute every Make-You-Happy Job Requirement exactly as written unless you find it does not meet or exceed expectations. If you find it no longer meets or exceeds expectations, take care of the customer. Then, take responsibility to change the MJR to what we and our customers need.
2. Participates with the President and other personnel in the development, implementation and updating of long term strategic and annual operational plans.
3. On an annual basis, develop the strategic goals and objectives for American Retail Supply Sales Department.
4. Oversee the achievement of the company's annual sales Objective.
5. On an annual basis, assign SMART (Specific, Measurable, Attainable, Relevant & Timed) objectives in areas of their job responsibilities for each of your direct reports.
6. Throughout the year, on a routine basis, take the necessary action required to assure that all reports are on target to achieve their annual objectives or take the corrective action necessary to get them on target.
7. Establishes a man/women power inventory by maintaining a continuous recruiting program for the strategic purpose of upgrading the caliber and productivity of employees in the sales organization.

81

8. Analyzes sales statistics to formulate policy and promote sales.

You get the idea. For our Vice President of Sales, the Job Description includes 31 more duties.

Objectives come directly from the Job Description. All objectives need to be S.M.A.R.T.

Specific - Objectives need to be specific. They need to be clear. Use exact numbers, dates, times, etc. State exactly what you want to accomplish. Who, what, where, and why.

Measurable – Objectives need to be measurable and big objectives need measurements along the way to achieving them. How will you demonstrate and evaluate the extent to which the objective has been accomplished?

Attainable - Objectives need to be realistic and attainable. While goals should stretch you and your team, they need to be realistic. It's often helpful to break a big objective into smaller objectives, so that you can continuously see progress that will keep you motivated to keep pushing forward.

Relevant – Objectives need to be relevant to the job description and getting the job done. The objective needs to tie into the key responsibilities of the job.

<u>Timed</u> – Objectives need to have a deadline, or timeframe for achieving your objective. Again, it's often helpful to break a big objective into smaller objectives with specific deadlines.

Here are the objectives for our Vice President of Sales. Notice, the first objective is to follow MJRs, identify deficiencies and correct the deficiencies.

Objectives
Vice President of Sales

- So that our business continually improves and we meet or exceed our internal and external customer expectations, execute every Make-You-Happy Job Requirement exactly as written unless you find it does not meet or exceed expectations. If you find it no longer meets or exceeds expectations, take care of the customer. Then, take responsibility to change the MJR to what we and our customers need.
- On a continuous basis, maintain and update the company training manual. Train sales skills, product knowledge, and computer skills as it pertains to the sales department. Implement, participate and encourage those in the sales department in continual learning about the job, the industry, management, marketing, & sales techniques.
- Meet with each staff member within the sales department for scheduled PDI's (Personal Development Interviews) to increase skills, meet their goals and help motivate them to become the best they can be at their jobs.
- Attend Personal Development Interviews with the CEO for the purpose of measuring progress toward objectives, reinforcement, and development. Collaborate on the sales department role, rules and overall direction.
- On a monthly basis, conduct routine sales meetings which are oriented around the three "I's" of meetings (Instructional,

Informational, and Inspirational) that are pertinent to sales. Invite speakers, record meetings and distribute materials and recordings to other locations.

- Oversee and coordinate sample areas, showrooms, and tradeshows for the company. Develop processes for sending samples, trade show selling and showroom selling.
- Work with individual clients when called upon to help close sales, take care of specific client needs or in overflow situations.
- Maintain and write MJR's (Make You Happy Job Requirements) within the department. Use MAT's (Make You Happy Action Teams) as needed for development in areas of sales processes, satisfying client needs, reducing errors or eliminating future errors.

Again, you get the idea. The V.P. Sales has 27 more SMART objectives. Again, a lot of these do not need to be reported upon as they have become routine, and you can't possibly discuss all of them in every PDI.

Reportable Objectives - Our V.P. of Sales has 35 objectives. We can't possibly discuss all 34 objectives in our PDI's, so we need to narrow them down to 8-12 Reportable Objectives that we discuss in our weekly personal development interviews.

Vice President Sales
20xx Reportable Objectives

1. Identify Make-You-Happy Job Requirements, or other things that we do that are broken, deficient or otherwise do not meet or exceed our internal and external customer expectations and help fix them.
2. On a weekly basis, take some specific and reportable action designed to increase the average annual sales per customer from $xxx.xx for the year 20xx to $xxx.xx for the year 20xx.

3. On a weekly basis throughout the year 20xx, take some specific and reportable action designed to increase market share from xx,xxx customers to xx,xxx.

4. On a weekly basis, take some specific and reportable action designed to increase the average order from $xxx.xx for the year 20xx to $xxx.xx for the year 20xx.

5. On a weekly basis, analyze sales performance of individual sales reps and locations. Listen to and observe sales reps. Monitor sales orders, quotations and interactions with clients to assure accuracy and that our clients are treated in the way that we want them to be treated.

6. On a preplanned basis, conduct PDI's (Personal Development Interviews) with each of the reporting sales personnel for the purpose of measuring progress against objectives, taking corrective action, increasing skills, and helping them motivate themselves to become the best they can be at their jobs.

7. On a preplanned basis, attend a Personal Development Interview with the CEO for the purpose of measuring progress toward objectives, reinforcement, and development.

8. On a weekly basis, take some specific and reportable action to create a motivating environment throughout the company by catching people doing things right and reinforcing them for such actions.

9. With a focus towards achieving the company sales objective for 20xx, on a monthly basis, take specific and reportable action to assure that all reports are on target for achieving their annual objectives or take the corrective action necessary to get them on target.

10. By April 30, 20xx hire an additional Sales Rep.

Activity Log – Between each PDI, the individual being interviewed records the activities he has taken in each area on his activity log. Notice, the activity log emphasizes action and activity. **There should be enough room after each question for the interviewee to make notes for the activities.**

You want to be sure that every PDI starts on a positive note, so start each PDI with the question, "What went right since we last met?" This question is included on the Activity Log so the individual has time to think about it and report on something positive.

Even with this, sometimes the individual will say, "Nothing went right." It is your job to turn this around, and make it into a positive, or at a minimum, a learning experience. Your response to, "Nothing went right" should be, "Tell me what went wrong?"

After the individual answers, "What went wrong?" you then ask, "What did you learn from that?" You then need to make sure that this leads to learning something positive.

It's important that your managers understand that they often are not responsible for doing these activities, but are responsible for coaching their team so they are done.

Here's an example from the activity log below. Our VP of Sales has a reportable objective of, "On a weekly basis, take some specific and reportable action designed to increase the average annual sales per customer from $xxx.xx for the year 20xx to $xxx.xx for the year 20xx."

She can "do" things that lead to achieving that goal, or she can coach team members to do things to achieve the goal.

She could "do" something by creating a campaign that the sales reps could use to sell higher priced items, or research the addition of products to our product line. That's "her doing the thing."

Or she could report on what she did to coach a team member to achieve the goal. She could report that she identified that Jane is not making progress on increasing the average annual sales per customer, and what Jane and her are doing to correct the action.

Or she might report that Fred is doing a great job increasing the average annual sales per customer and we think it's because he's doing this and we've shared this with the rest of the team.

It's important for the manager to understand that they're not just reporting on what they do, but on what they do to coach their team.

Here is the Activity Log for our Vice President of Sales.

Vice President Sales
20xx Activity Log

1. What went right this week?
2. Report on sales objectives. Written and Shipped – Last 5 days, MTD, last 30 days and year-to-date.
3. Identify Make-You-Happy Job Requirements, or other things that we do that are broken, deficient or otherwise do not meet or exceed our internal and external customer expectations that I identified and helped to fix.
4. Action taken to increase the average annual sales per customer from $xxx.xx for the year 20xx to $xxx.xx for the year 20xx.
5. Action taken to increase market share from xx,xxx customers to xx,xxx.
6. Action taken to increase the average order from $xxx.xx for the year 20xx to $xxx.xx for the year 20xx.
7. Action taken to listen to and observe sales reps. Monitor sales orders, quotes and interactions with clients to assure accuracy and that our clients are treated in the way that we want them to be treated.

87

8. Action taken to conduct PDIs (Personal Development Interviews) with each of the reporting sales personnel for the purpose of measuring progress against objectives, taking corrective action, increasing skills, and helping them motivate themselves to become the best they can be at their jobs
9. Action taken to attend a Personal Development Interview with the CEO for the purpose of measuring progress toward objectives, reinforcement, and development.
10. Action taken to create a motivating environment throughout the company by catching people doing things right and reinforcing them for such actions.
11. Action taken to assure that all reports are on target for achieving their annual objectives or take the corrective action necessary to get them on target.
12. Action taken to hire an additional sales rep by April 30th, 20xx.
13. Actions not shown above.

Interview Guide - The interview guide is used by the manager as their guide for the interview. To create the interview guide, simply turn reportable objectives into questions. Be sure to add the questions, "What action did you take that we didn't talk about?" and "Is there anything else you want to talk about?" at the end of every interview.

You should leave enough room to write notes between each question. Writing notes show the interviewee that you're paying attention. It will also create some natural quiet time in which the interviewee will add to his responses and that's good. Writing notes will also help you with your summery at the end of your Personal Development Interview.

Suggestion – Write your notes in black or blue ink. If you ask a question that requires a follow up by either you or the interviewee, circle your note with a red pen and make sure you address these after the PDI or during the next PDI.

As we discussed earlier, PDIs should be very positive experiences for both the manager and the interviewee. This is where you'll catch people doing things right, reinforce that behavior, and create a positive growing business.

Vice President Sales
2011 Interview Guide

1. What went right this week?
2. How did we do on our sales objectives since we last met? Written and Shipped – Last 5 days, MTF, last 30 days, year-to-date.
3. What Make-You-Happy Job Requirements or other things we do did you identify that are broken, deficient, or otherwise do not meet or exceed our internal and external customer expectations? What did you do to fix it?
4. What action did you, or your reports take to increase the average annual sales per customer from $x,xxx for the year 20xx to $x,xxx for the year 20xx?
5. What action did you, or your reports, take to increase the market share from xx,xxx customers to xx,xxx?
6. What action did you, or your reports, take to increase the average order from $xxx for the year 20xx to $xxx for the year 20xx.
7. What action did you take to listen to and observe sales reps and monitor sales orders, quotations and interactions with clients to assure accuracy and that our clients are treated in the way we want them treated?
8. What action did you take to conduct PDIs (Personal Development Interviews) with each of the reporting sales personnel for the purpose of measuring progress against objectives, taking corrective action, increasing skills, and

helping them motivate themselves to become the best they can be at their jobs?

9. What action did you take to attend a Personal Development Interview with the CEO for the purpose of measuring progress toward objectives, reinforce, and development?

10. What action did you take to create a motivating environment throughout the company by catching people doing things right and reinforcing them for such actions.

11. What action did you take to assure that all reports are on target for achieving their annual objective, or what action did you take to get them on target?

12. What action did you take to hire an additional sale rep by April 30th, 20xx?

13. What actions did you take that are not shown above?

14. Is there anything else you would like to discuss?

PDI Summary: One of the best parts of your PDI is the summery. Use the notes you've taken to summarize what has been accomplished. This is incredibly motivating for both the interviewer and the interviewee. You'll summarize what's been discussed in the interview and every time the manager and the interviewee leave pumped up and ready to take on the world.

The management system detailed in the back of this book provides JORIAs for **214 different job positions** including:

Company President	Vice President Information Services
Purchasing Manager	Sales Representative
Vice President Operations	Vice President Sales
Warehouse Manager	Accounts Payable
Accounts Receivable	Administrative Assistant
Branch Manager	Assistant Branch Manager
Call Center Manager	Clerical Administrative Assistant
Closing Manager	Computer System Coordinator
Controller	Dispatcher

Delivery Driver
Director of Client Services
Loan Service Manager
Payroll Clerk
Plant Manager
Purchasing Manager
Shop Manager
Warehouse Crew
Accounting Assistant
Cashier
Chief Operating Officer
Customer Service Director
Director of Advertising
Director of MIS
Executive Secretary
Greeter
Field Manager
Foreman
Team Leader
Parts Manager
Receptionist
Service Technician
Shipper
Shipping Supervisor
Treasurer
Triage Nurse
Medical Director
Dental Director
Nurse
Physician's Assistant

Deputy Director
Vice President Marketing
Manager - Accounting Department
Plant Manager
Purchaser
Regional Manager
Buyer
Bookkeeper
Billing Clerk
Chief Financial Officer
Collections Manager
Customer Service Representative
Store Manager
Equipment Manager
General Manager
Human Resources Director
Operations Manager
Loan Officer
Office Manager
Project Manager
Sales Support Assistant
Service Writer
Shipping and Receiving Manager
Systems Administrator
Vice President Customer Service
Dentist
Assistant Medical Director
Medical Assistant
Physician

We've discussed 2 of the 3 components that you need to take control of your business and your life. The third is critical because regardless of the systems you have in place for your business or the Performance Feedback System you have if you don't have the third component, your business will be mediocre at best. Read on to learn more about the third component.

CHAPTER 17
How to Implement Customer Service That Gets Customers Coming Back Time and Time Again and Enthusiastically Telling Their Friends About You

We see our customer as invited guests to a party and we are the hosts. It's our job every day to make every important aspect of the customer experience a little bit better.
Jeff Bezos, CEO – Amazon.com

As the author of *The Happy Customer Handbook, 59 Secrets to Creating Happy Customers Who Come Back Time and Time Again and Enthusiastically Tell Others About You* I am often asked, "What is the number one thing business owners can do to improve their customer service?" Another question I get is, "Why is customer service so poor?"

When I speak to live audiences I often ask this question, "What should you be doing when it comes to customer service training in your business?"

A. We tell our staff to deliver good customer service. They should know what that is.
B. We tell our staff to deliver good customer service and give some examples sometimes, but nothing formal.
C. We have meetings about customer service once in a while and tell everyone they should give good customer service.
D. All new staff gets customer service training when they are hired.
E. Everyone has gone through our customer service training

and they are consistently and persistently reminded about our customer service expectations.

F. With every audience, almost all hands go up for answer E. Their customer service training should be, everyone has gone through our customer service training and they are consistently and persistently reminded about our customer service expectations.

At www.TheHappyCustomerHandbook.com, we've surveyed thousands of business owners before they purchase *The Happy Customer Handbook*. We ask them: What best describes customer service training in your organization?

A. We tell our staff to deliver good customer service. They should know what that is.
B. We tell our staff to deliver good customer service and give some examples sometimes, but nothing formal.
C. We have meetings about customer service once in a while and tell everyone they should give good customer service.
D. All new staff gets customer service training when they are hired.
E. Everyone has gone through our customer service training and they are consistently and persistently reminded about our customer service expectations.

Only 2% answer E - Why is that? Why is it that everyone knows their team should have consistent customer training up front and consistent reminders, but almost no one does it?

Here's why: With the best of intentions, the business owner

has a "rah rah" meeting about customer service and the service improves for a few weeks. Then, without reminders, you're back where you started. And the reason is simple: **the reminders don't come because you're a busy business owner and you have a lot of other things to do.**

In addition, you're a 5-percenter and can't understand why people don't always do what they're supposed to do.

But this may even be more amazing. More than 75% of all businesses have no upfront customer service training for new employees.

The answer to the questions, "What can business owners do to improve their customer service?" and "Why is customer service so poor?" is the same:

1. Train your entire team to deliver exceptional customer service.
2. Consistently reinforce your customer service expectations with your team.

To start, your entire team needs to get trained with your exceptional customer service expectations. This is the "rah, rah" training I talked about above. **But it can't stop there!**

You need to consistently and persistently reinforce those expectations. Zig Ziglar says, "Repetition is the mother of all learning." But learning something doesn't necessarily lead to behavior change, so when it comes to customer service in your business I say, "Repetition is the mother of all learning **and permanent behavior change."**

Now that you have your entire team trained and you're consistently reminding them about your customer service expectations, what happens when you get a new employee (team member)? You need to make sure every new employee gets the exact same initial customer service training that your entire team received.

You Never Have a Second Chance
to Make a First Impression

The best thing you can do to show your commitment to exceptional customer service for every new employee is to train them with your customer service expectations immediately. After your new team member fills out the required government employment forms, what do they do? In most businesses, it's not customer service training, but it should be. Whether you create your own training, use the training we have available at www.KeithLee.com, or invest in other training system, be sure that the very first training every new employee receives is customer service.

Regardless of how well you implement the Systems, Employee Empowerment, and Performance Management with Personal Development Interviews discussed in this book, if you're not committed to exceptional customer service then your business will be mediocre at best.

When the Cat's Away...

The very best customer service that any customer will ever get in your business is when you're there, right next to your employee. At that point, if you accept "good," the service when you're not around will, without question, be **less than good**. That's **not good** for the health of your business.

When you're committed to exceptional customer service, you'll fall short sometimes. But when you do, you'll often still be providing good customer service. In addition, when your customers are used to getting exceptional customer service they'll be much more likely to forgive you in the rare instance when your customer service falls below good.

That doesn't mean they won't complain when your service falls below good, but that's great!

I love customers who complain. Complaints give us an opportunity to improve on the Systems we created previously and the opportunity to WOW our customer with the solution to their complaint.

The reality is that the huge majority of customers who are disappointed with any business won't complain to anyone, they just leave. How does that sound to you? "They just leave." That should send chills through your blood.

It's reported that for every twenty-five dissatisfied customers, only one complains. Twenty-four don't complain and on average the non-complainers tell 10 to 20 other people.

On the other hand, in the Harvard Business Review, Frederick F. Reichheld and W. Earl Sasser, Jr report that a 5% increase in customer loyalty can produce profit increases of 25% to 85%. With numbers like these, you have to love customers who complain because they give you a chance to make them happy, and fix your systems.

You'll never achieve a high level of customer service unless your expectations for customer service are extraordinary.

Secret Number 3 in my book *The Happy Customer Handbook, 59 Secrets to Creating Happy Customers Who Come Back Time and Time Again and Enthusiastically Tell Others*

About You is, "Your customer service expectations need to be extraordinary."

My mom worked for Sears when I was growing up. For years, maybe decades, their motto was, "Satisfaction Guaranteed." Where did that get them? Customer satisfaction isn't enough.

Satisfied customers are... satisfied. If someone else has a little better price, or is a bit more convenient, they're gone. Just think of it. If your goal is a satisfied customer, even if you and your staff do everything perfectly, the best you'll get is a satisfied customer.

Customer satisfaction is not good enough. Your customer service expectations need to be exceptional, and you need to create not only satisfied customers, but happy and loyal customers as well.

When I say loyal customers I don't mean customers who stay with you for some nebulous, touchy-feely reasons. They are loyal for specific reasons; your product knowledge, advice, product mix, and they know you'll always take care of them. They know you won't oversell them (think auto repair), and they know they'll always see a smiling face or receive a pleasant greeting. They know they can expect to get a sincere thank you, and be SERVED with an attitude of sincere appreciation. They know they will never be promised something you don't really think you can deliver... the list goes on and on.

What happens when a happy, loyal customer finds a lower price? They're likely to stay with you, or at least let you know. What happens when a competitor, who's a bit more convenient, moves in, and your customer is happy and loyal? They'll keep coming back to you.

What happens when you mess up with a happy, loyal customer? Your happy, loyal customer knows that's not normal, and they're likely to tell you and let you make it right.

What happens when the subject of the products or services you offer comes up with a happy, loyal customer? They're likely to rave about you and you're likely to get another new customer.

As you can see, *The Happy Customer Handbook, 59 Secrets to Creating Happy Customers Who Come Back Time and Time Again and Enthusiastically Tell Others About You* is not an ordinary, "same-as-every-other" customer service book. It is a quick and easy read with ideas you can use every day to **Create Happy Customers Who Come Back Time and Time Again and Enthusiastically Tell Others About You.** Readers of this book can get a free copy of *The Happy Customer Handbook* at www.TheHappyCustomerHandbook.com.

CHAPTER 18
Putting It All Together

As I mentioned early in the book, at the urging of business associates who've owned their own businesses, I modified my management system to be quickly and easily implemented and make it available to business owners like you. I wanted it to be as simple to implement as possible in as short amount of time as possible. All you need to do is follow the easy step-by-step instructions and you will never again be one of those business owners moaning and complaining about your staff.

You'll implement the Make-You-Happy Management System over three months. Why a three-month implementation?

- Your team and you need time to change. While this is a very easy, virtually done-for-you system, it is comprehensive and involves significant changes for both you and your team. Neither you, nor your team, can change this much overnight.

- Plus you need to show your team that this isn't just your newest fad. When you introduce the system your team is going to sit back, smile and nod yes, while thinking...

This Too Will Pass...

We've seen it before. This is just the newest thing he's brought back from a seminar. We'll just smile and nod; and **this too will pass.** You need to show them that this too will **not** pass, and the only way to do that is with your actions - over time.

- In addition, three months makes sense. This is a 3-Step

Done-For-You System:
1. Creating Make-You-Happy Customer Service.
2. Creating Systems and Team Member Empowerment.
3. Eliminating Performance Reviews and replacing them with Personal Development Interviews.

Month 1
Make-You-Happy Customer Service Training System

- **Make-You-Happy Customer Service Training DVD -** In this DVD your team will learn what Make-You-Happy Customer Service is, and how to deliver it every time so your customers come back time after time and enthusiastically tell others about you. It includes the leader's guide, workbook, and answer key. The leader's guide will show you step-by-step exactly how to conduct your meeting. Your team will answer the questions in the workbook to ensure their understanding of Make-You-Happy Customer Service.

- **Make-You-Happy New Employee Customer Service Training DVD -** It is absolutely critical that every new employee receives the exact same customer service training that your team received. If you really want your team to understand your commitment to Make-You-Happy Customer Service, then this needs to be the very first training every new team member gets. No computer training, no "how to get email" training, no instructions about stocking shelves... no nothing until they understand your commitment to exceptional customer service. This training includes your Leader's Guide and Workbook for the new team member to complete as he/she watches the DVD. It also includes the answer key to the workbook.

- **Ongoing Training Guidelines -** Almost all customer service training fails for the same reason. There is no consistent and persistent ongoing customer service training reinforcement. You'll use these guidelines to deliver consistent and persistent ongoing customer service training over time.
- **Fast Start Guide -** These step-by-step instructions insure that you get Make-You-Happy Customer Service implemented fast.

Month 2

Creating Systems and Team Member Empowerment

- **Make-You-Happy Management System Training DVD** Your team has already seen that you're committed to a new level of customer service. Now it's time to watch the Management System Training DVD and show them your new Management System that they'll love. Simply follow the leaders guide when you train your team in your new Management System that gets Buy-In from them, creates wealth for you, allows your team to continue to improve daily whether you have turnover or not, and sets you free!
- **Make-You-Happy New Employee Management System Training DVD -** Now that your entire team is trained in your new management system, you need to be sure that every new employee gets the same training. And now that you've implemented the Make-You-Happy Management System training system, training for new employees is **systemized** also. When you hire a new team member, the first training they'll get is on customer service.

Immediately after each new employee watches the Make-You-Happy New Employee Customer Service Training DVD, they will watch the Make-You-Happy Management System DVD and complete the workbook. From then on, they will know they are expected to use both their brain and their brawn. You will never hear anyone say, "I didn't think I could," or "I didn't think I should," or "I didn't think..."

- **Step-By-Step Procedure to Create Your First 3 Systems in 9 Minutes -** Remember, a System is simply writing down how you do a particular job. You'll easily use "as-is" or tweak the systems included, that are used by almost every business, to create your first 3 systems in 9 minutes.

- **Step-By-Step Procedure to Create 2 Systems for Every Position in Your Business in Less Than 2 Hours -** You'll simply go through the scores of "Systems" used by other businesses to do the same jobs you do in your business, tweak them a bit, and they're ready to go in your business.

- **Step-By-Step Procedure to Turn Your Team Into a System Creating Machine That Generates All of the Systems You Need -** After watching the training DVD you'll show your team how you quickly and easily created two Systems for every position in your business. You'll ask them to edit the Systems you've created (empowerment!) and then use the rest of the Systems included to create all of the systems needed for their position.

- **Guide to Systems and Empowerment Manual -** Systems alone aren't enough. You need Buy-In from your team. You need everyone on your team working to make your business better every day by improving your Systems.

You need help from your team. Unless you want to be the King Solomon of your business and be responsible for every improvement and every decision, this guide will give you knowledge and resources to implement systems and empowerment in your business in no time.

Month 3
Performance Management through Personal Development Interviews

- **Performance Management -** You know you need to manage the performance of your team but you likely have no system to do it because you know Performance Reviews are demotivating, demoralizing, and counterproductive and you don't know what else to do. You'll learn how to replace Performance Reviews with motivating and productive Personal Development Interviews.

- **DVD Training to Teach You and Your Managers How to Implement Personal Development Interviews -** 3 DVDs that show you and your managers exactly how to conduct Personal Development Interviews with everyone on your team. You'll learn how to master the Personal Development Interview so that every manager and subordinate leaves pumped-up, ready to take on the world after every interview.

- **8 Audio CDs with 8 Real PDI's, Including an Evaluation of each by Keith Lee -** Listen as Keith interviews the president of one of his businesses, and 3 vice presidents. You'll also hear 4 managers conducting Personal Development Interviews with their team members. Each interview includes a written evaluation by Keith. You'll see and hear for yourself exactly how a Personal Development

Interview should be conducted.

- **Personal Development Interview Evaluation Forms -** You'll want to record some of your interviews with your managers and evaluate yourself. You'll also want your managers to record their interviews. Both of you will then listen to the interview and fill out the evaluation form. This is an incredible training tool.

Special Bonuses

While the following are not critical to implementing the Make-You-Happy Management System, they are great resources that you'll want to use in your business.

.

- **Conflict Resolution -** Do you ever have personal conflict in your business? I'm not talking about the healthy conflict of legitimate ideas, concepts, strategies, or tactics; I mean personal conflict. Immediately upon distributing this three page Conflict Resolution Guideline, personal conflict will drop by at least 75%. When your team knows that they'll actually be responsible for solving their conflict using these guidelines, they'll put on their big boy, or girl, panties and learn how to get along... and some of your biggest complainers will simply move on.
- **Hiring Top Performers -** With this system, you'll take the guess work out of hiring. We've been using this system for about 10 years and we'll NEVER hire another person without using it. You'll stop relying on gut and start using proven scientific hiring practices.
- **Employee Handbook -** You'll get a copy of the employee

handbook we use in our businesses with offices in four states. Even if you have a well-written, legal, human resources approved employee handbook, you'll likely get ideas from this for your business. You, of course, should have your attorney review your employee handbook before you implement it.

As I mentioned at the beginning of this book, You Will Take TOTAL Control of Your Business When You Create Systems to Control Your Business. But I also asked, Who Has Time To Create Those Systems?

That's what the Make-You-Happy Management System is all about; giving you systems that you can tweak to take total control over your business.

Remember...

"All wealth is based on systems."

Dan Kennedy

"Let systems run the business and people run the systems. People come and go, but systems remain constant."

Michael Gerber

"For the business owner, systems set you free."

Keith Lee

To discover even more about How to Control Your Business and Your Life go to www.KeithLee.com to get the Make-You-Happy Management System and Create Your Highly Productive Team.